HOW MEN PRAY

FLORIDA POETRY SERIES

2005

*Mary Dell —
Roots! Enjoy
our roots!! And
great to
meet you.*

HOW MEN PRAY

POEMS

Philip F. Deaver

Philip F. Deaver

FLORIDA POETRY SERIES

2005

4/27/005

Cover art: *Pair of Squash,* 1988 by James B. Moore
Author photo: Anitra Green
Cover design, book design, and production: C. L. Knight
Typesetting: titles set in Tiepolo; text set in Galliard

Library of Congress Cataloging-in-Publication Data
How Men Pray by Philip F. Deaver – First Edition
ISBN 0938078-82-8 (paper)
Library of Congress Cataloging Card Number – 2005900047

This publication is sponsored in part by a grant
from the Florida Department of State,
Division of Cultural Affairs, and the Florida Arts Council.

Anhinga Press Inc. is a nonprofit corporation dedicated wholly
to the publication and appreciation of fine poetry.

For personal orders, catalogs and information write to:
Anhinga Press
P.O. Box 10595
Tallahassee, Florida 32302
Web site: www.anhinga.org
E-mail: info@anhinga.org

Published in the United States
by Anhinga Press
Tallahassee, Florida
First Edition, 2005

In memory of my mom and dad,
Philip and Althea

CONTENTS

ACKNOWLEDGMENTS

"Fossils" first appeared in *The Reaper* and was reprinted in *Florida in Poetry*. "Shoney's" and "Corona" were published in the *Florida Review*. "The Night Light in the New Life" was published by *Poetry Miscellany*. The poem "Okay" appeared in the special editors issue of *Measure*, the creative writing magazine of St. Joseph's College.

The epigraph for "Michael at Twelve" is from the poem, "A Happy Childhood," by William Matthews, used by permission of William Matthews.

Special thanks to Lynne Knight for her patience and careful editing, and to Rollins College for the Critchfield Grant that twice made writing possible. Thanks also to my friend and poetry mentor Russ Kesler, to my long-time friend Herb Budden, and to Rick Campbell, Mark Jarman, Lezlie Laws, David Huddle, Pat James, Kelle Groome, Richard Jackson, Ken Smith, Carol Frost, Gianna Russo, Suzannah Gilman, Paul Freidinger, Tamra Hays, Kären Blumenthal, Lisa Ryan Musgrave, and, of course, Susan Lilley.

In addition, I must acknowledge the valued friendship over many years of the poet William Matthews. I'm among the many whom he inspired and cared to help.

HOW MEN PRAY

ONE

YOUR MARS LOOMING

Your Mars was looming before dawn this morning
at your west horizon of your overbig sky; from here on
it will fade. The planet was amber. Your silence prevailed.

All things seemed to observe the moment. Even the dog
paused to look, in dewy grass, elbow deep, at the edge
of the lake's flat black water. Your day was just beginning.

Yesterday at our same time Mars was higher
in a slightly brighter sky. The days are getting shorter.
When I first began watching, last month, longest days,

heat of summer, the moon passed over ahead of Mars;
but during the month Mars left it far behind, the moon
in its nightly phases, in a big cool orbit of its own,

and Venus and Saturn splayed and went their different ways
and while the big dipper kept its shape, it pivoted and twirled
like a kite hooked to Polaris which remained at your North

as if pinned there. What a living thing your night sky is.
In its hours between the light, we might think it passes
in formation. No. Your synchrony is far bigger than that.

THE VANISHING POINT

for Jeanne Schubert

See how the lines of this picture
seem to pull the two figures
along a rail receding to the distance?
See how the trees
and rocks along the Colorado River too are pulled?
It's a long shot, so there's depth, panorama
and vast opportunity. My dad's hand
is on my shoulder but can't remain there
and I'm too young to know it.
See the way his eyes
stare directly into the camera? He's waiting
for the flutter behind the lense
that signals the moment is over.

Family vacation, 1963,
a year before the wreck,
and even today I feel that hand on my shoulder,
not as in a dream or my imagination
but in the most real of ways.
In the rigid zone that is the difference
between photograph and reality,
I look for the ghost of some hovering premonition
we hadn't noticed before —
a predictive configuration in the clouds,
or a warning in the haze and shadow in the trees
or in the flash of the river passing just behind us.

What I find
is what we find in any picture
locked in these dimensions —
the vanishing point —
operating on us both and equally, like gravity and
that day's now forgotten weather —
pulling us away from there and then and here and now,
toward a small hole in the firmament where
even a couple of guys running all too parallel might —
and this is a *real* long shot —
meet again.

DOPPLER

The effect of coming on
in reverse —
that is, the effect of fading
after having come on already.
I recall my father's scent
in rooms of our house
the day he died. He'd showered and shaved
before he left, and there was that.
But also the smell of him
was in the book on the table,
was on the window sill
where he'd set his ben franklin glasses,
was near a dish he'd carried upstairs,
was in a basket of his laundry;
was along the upstairs hall
trapped in dead air; was in the crossbreezes
and pulled out of hanging clothes by the attic fan,
by the torque of summer heat,
by me touching his stuff to my face.
The smell was fading from the moment
I noticed it — as if something in the air knew
he wouldn't return to reinforce it this time;
as if something in the very air knew
he didn't exist anymore. They were orphan smells.
I don't recall going into the drawers and shelves,
the cabinets and closets, the bookcases and the garage
and the basement and cistern and the floor registers
and the grass in the yard, going all the places we had
to go to finally remove him, but in a few weeks
he was entirely gone.

NAME RECOGNITION

I have a persistent image of the past
as a grave we stare up out of
so we can easily see the sky
and the clouds passing in their varied moods —
but old friends, in their separate holes,
cannot see us;
so there's no real sadness
that you didn't remember my face
because for me the past is a death already
but I'm glad you remembered my name.

GRAY

This was our pretty gray kitten,
hence her name; who was born
in our garage and stayed nearby
her whole life. There were allergies;
so she was, as they say,
an outside cat.
But she loved us. For years,
she was at our window.
Sometimes, a paw on the screen
as if to want in, as if
to be with us
the best she could.
She would be on the deck,
at the sliding door.
She would be on the small
sill of the window in the bathroom.
She would be at the kitchen
window above the sink.
We'd go to the living room;
anticipating that she'd be there, too,
hop up, look in.
She'd be on the roof,
she'd be in a nearby tree.
She'd be listening
through the wall to our family life.
She knew where we were,
and she knew where we were going
and would meet us there.
Little spark of consciousness,
calm kitty eyes staring
through the window.

After the family broke,
and when the house was about to sell,
I walked around it for a last look.
Under the eaves, on the ground,
there was a path worn in the dirt,
tight against the foundation –
small padded feet, year after year,
window to window.

When we moved, we left her
to be fed by the people next door.
Months after we were gone,
they found her in the bushes
and buried her by the fence.
So many years after,
I can't get her out of my mind.

OTTO AND FORGETTING

I forget the first part,
but eventually the rutted road
from Otto comes to the old farm,
turns right and stays flat to the bridge,
then goes up.
But I come the other way,
walk down from the top.
The road is gravel on dirt, big gravel,
rough going on the steepest slopes.
When a pickup hurries by,
it crosses my mind to ask for a ride
but no.

Viewed from behind,
the farmer's hound's beagle butt
is tireless in its waddling style of going up.
He is accustomed.
He needs no hickory walking stick
or place to lean sometimes and catch his breath.
He runs ahead, chasing deer from the road
before I round the curves.
He looks back: "C'mon!" he's saying.
Sometimes he runs a rabbit into the brush,
but then he's back, and still I've not caught up.
I rest in a shady draw.
I forget where I am in the journey.

Up top at Bearfoot Lodge, this very spot,
visible through oak tree tops as
one notch in the hitch of a switchback,
seems miles below.
You lean way over the porch rail to see it.

That's me down there. I've walked down
and now I'm walking back up.
I forget why.

OKAY

I don't like the shortening of the days,
the year's desultory autumn decline.
But November 15,
coming down the street into morning sun,
the lake calm in a white shroud of mist,
I smile awake and warm to possibilities.
The day begins damp. It will be cool.
Suddenly I'm happy.
A night's sleep under my belt,
I can handle all there is to do and the more
there is to do after that. Circumstance
hasn't yet tied its first knot in me,
and a lot of things I usually think of
haven't come to mind yet.
Okay, it's an illusion. But the sun
is just above horizontal to the flat plain of water,
the sky rose red to the east,
calming to dark blue above;
the lake is poised and pending, the green
surrounding the water is primordial friends with it,
the cypress knees up from mud
with all the optimism of a real tree.
Everything seems to know
that everything will be fine.
From now on I'll go to work every morning by this route.
It will be daily mass, but instead of homily,
I'll have coming-on sunlight over new paradise,
a prayer for peace and calm.
Okay. I'll dive in. I can. Like the anhinga
I see swimming by the dock,
I can dry my wings later.

USED

Through the front window tonight, I see
an old car of mine across the street,
its owner visiting neighbors, I guess.
I look close, thinking surely not. I dress,
go out — really have to — walk around it,
imagining what I'll say if they see me.
The blue's faded by exactly the number of years
since I last saw it — three — at a lot south of town
where I unloaded it for cash
on one of those peculiar winter afternoons
when there seemed no other way.
I'll bet the familiar steering wheel
still has my DNA — particle of hide from my hand,
bit of eyelash. The windows seem darker,
like the house you used to live in but don't anymore.
The dash is cleaner than I kept it.
There's a weathered bumper decal I disagree with
that came later. My old car's moved on without me.
I bought it used, kept it ten years.
Vacuumed it on Saturday afternoons
at the Mobil and changed the oil
at 3000 miles. I morbidly regretted
spilled coffee, monitored the gradual
demise of the wiper blades, and listened
for the arrival of the end in the whir
of the old transmission.
I worried about the paint
and the old tires growing slick,
and the headliner's sag.
The ding that's still there
where the shopping cart
tagged it, winter of the fifth year,
got five years of my futile best intentions
to get it pounded out.

I can still remember the feel of the ride,
anonymous out there in the long bumper to bumper,
it and me, a team rolling north on the interstate,
bags in the trunk, tent and typewriter,
books in the back seat, blankets, a coat —
younger, on the road, everything fine;
the speakers in the rear blown
but the ones in front strong.
Coffee, Chrissie Hynde on tape, 77 mph on cruise,
the fabric of the seats a used gray blue,
nondescript but optimistic,
exactly like me.

ME IN ROY'S OLD OFFICE

All these moods that bend over me,
his shadowy marked and marked-in books,
the hanger for his coat,

the squeak in this funky desk chair,
and all these voices in the hall
that I hear through his old glass door —

all of it he left behind. Keys and small change
in the desk drawers, ballpoints that still write,
and, piled on the desk, his tortured collection

of Blake. I'm here now. Like I've come upon
an abandoned camp, and the coffee's still
giving wisps of steam and the coals are warm,

but the tent's gone, and the bedroll and the horse.
It's mine now, the note says. I lean back
and take in the air of this strange room

and try to conjure him so I can ask
what he knew and why he left like that
and whether, indeed, I'm as lucky as I think.

WOUNDED KNEE

I send this to you who don't hear me
by normal means
and who will never read it,
from this hill where I, the traveler, stand,
where our warring ancestors are buried —
I send it down toward you from the arched iron gate
of the white man's cemetery,
down the hill to the rough roadside lean-to
where on this day, with a storm
looming dark blue beyond the upwind bluffs,
you sit alone, eagle feather in your hair,
selling dream-catchers to tourists
if only there were any. Catch this:
even anglo honky white boys from Illinois
live with stuff. I'm sorry. I send this
down the long grassy slope to the road,
across the powdery dirt made up of your dead
prairie people, the slaughtered buffalo, the dead eagle —
I send it into the shadows of the shelter
where you sit staring up at me.
I send it to you some other way than calling to you,
stormy day daydream, rolling rock, mental telepathy,
smoke signals, the posture of how men pray.

THE TRAIN ALONG THE TOE

At night on the Penland ridge in the second week,
I'm lonely again; from the loft
the cabin stretches away in all directions;
the stirring sounds isolate me —
of the mice skittering past my traps
in the cabinet beneath the sink,
of the nightbirds and wheezing crickets
in the llama field nearby, of the soaring mountain
wind lifting through the pine stand;
but then, 3:28, the train
loaded down with gravel labors through, pulling
for a while, then on the downhill holding
back, the air brakes' unworldly song bouncing
off the flat-flowing river Toe and rising up a dark
hillside of shadow pine and moon poplar.
I lie near the window, the candle out,
my face as close to the screen as I can get it.
I pray for sleep before the silence comes again.
The last car, still far away, is rumbling up the hill and
rounding the curve from Spruce Pine to Penland Post,
but the engine's whistle, far in the future, is calling
already to Newdale bridge and Burnsville crossing.
I breathe in the interrupted air.
I'm calling forward, too. "I'm up here!" I shout
into the dark of my new dream, and I am.

ALTHEA

There was a grand piano and a couch
in the large front room of the Illinois house
and a formal staircase, a double flight
with switchback that led up into the shadows
where I lurked out of sight and
listened to my mother play.

When I think of her now, I remember
all the work she did. She was being 1950s good.
She looked real nice and kept a smile.
She cleaned and made the beds
and ironed the white shirts, and she
put food on the table at the appointed time.

She had long thin fingers, long nails hard and red.
In the pause of mid-afternoon on a summer day,
she came to the piano bench, sat a moment
(I could hear the pages of the songbook turn),
and then she warmed to something with a few runs
of the right hand, nails clicking on the ivory.

She had two kids, probably just down the street,
her husband wasn't due home 'til six;
The house smelled of starch and soap and food.
I don't know what her dreams were
but she was still young and she still had them
and for a moment the work was done and

just right then, sky blue above, jays
sweeping through the yard, town leaning
toward evening, friends busy somewhere else,
there was a sigh and clearing of the throat

that meant she was blissfully alone and
things were 1950s fine so far
as either of us
separately
knew.

DAWNING

The morning is slow to dawn,
clouds hanging low to the tops of trees
and cars move along the streets.
Blocks away and over there, the sea pounds,
white noise. The day has finally come.

Across the low plain outside of town
and north of the last house going that way,
and beyond the wilderness we overlooked
to the west, and east out into the ocean,
I listen. The clock turns. Sea birds wind

above the waves, and town birds shift
to the wires. Down my block a cat
crouches in his little yard. I move
to get ready. Up some tall stairs
and into another life, you are waiting.

If the music is off
you can feel the same morning I do.
If the music is on,
you'll feel it soon anyway.

LAC SEUL

Good morning to you, Lac Seul,
after so many years away.
I found my way back to you
in sleep but feel it all.
We'd motor out into the fog
in the cold June dawn, 1957.
We'd find an inlet and fish for hours,
pools turning, twist of currents,
not a word said. We'd build our fire
at noon for lunch, pike and beans,
scrape it all away like it never happened,
climb back in the boat and fish till dusk.
So many years after your lapping clear water,
your silent pines and rock ledges,
your afternoons with the moose moving
in the black shadows of your woods nearby,
your cold nights with the bears;
the Indian guide, Charlie, in the corner
of the cabin away from the woodstove,
watching in another language.
Lac Seul, what a gift you were, dream
and home movie, earliest initiation,
first utter absence of my mother,
tan hard skrim of my father in blood sport,
storms.

EQUINOX

Last night, a Cardinal game
was on TV. St. Louis is in the distant
but still familiar latitudes of home,
and the announcer happened to mention
it was expected to be in the forties;
welcome, autumn, please be brisk.

I know the Illinois air at this time,
how it hangs from the light like a veil,
blue-gray and rosey red, and haze.
There's a town there called "Haze,"
but it's spelled "Hays," I think,
but anyway I know how the light is

and how, because Illinois is laid out on a grid,
the sun at equinox rises and sets precisely
on the east-west streets and roads,
blazing down the highway centerline
as if it were taking aim. We think back on
home because we're lonely; we took in that

air in our early lives, and it took us in.
Illinois is still back there for us; in summer
on the map of our lives, it drifts and
memories swirl, voices, birds, haze, hot,
but at equinox Illinois links up once more
with earth and stars, and the sun marks its spot.

SWITCH ENGINES

In the night, five blocks away
under a high dome of clear sky,
the switch engines are working —
Illinois Central, Baltimore and Ohio —
you can hear them idling, the big diesels,
or, steel on steel you can hear them
make their switching runs — like
enormous gray bricks on edge,
they slide clear of the town lights,
wide of the highway overpass and the dark river,
and there they wait;
and maybe then you can hear the switchman
throw the hydraulic switch, maybe
you can hear the hydraulic clank
of the moveable rail;
then on signal the engine runs back in, renewed,
fifteen feet further north
on a track that can get him to Detroit
whereas the other one, seemingly parallel,
would run him into Indy
a few blocks south of Washington Street
where the medium tall buildings stand
in their own shadows, cold concrete,
2 a.m., 1961,
waiting for some future Republican
to build convention facilities, but

In my bed I listen to the switch engines,
out in the big wide world — my town
is only one mile square, a village, an outpost,
yet for me, of course, it's the center —
my mother's sleeping beside my father
        in the next room,

and my dog in the long yard, vigilant,
stares into the flickering streetlight,
filtered through lilac bushes disturbed
right then by the nightwind, and
my sister in her bed, in a room
seemingly parallel to mine,
will land five hundred miles away
in Memphis twenty years hence.

Take
all the rain
that will fall in the Spring
on this town and the big flat fields
that surround it, take
all the sunlight that will ache down
on silent afternoons the year the dioxins
gurgle up, the year the paint
chips off the houses, the year the bank
collapses because of farm loans,
the year the radiation from Chernobyl
        spins around the globe, and

Take
the park and Main Street
as I remember them in my childhood,
the gray men of the community in baggy pants
and pulled down hats — remembered like
wax statues in the frozen postures
of 1950's responsibility — take
the echoes of their ageless chatter
in the barber's chair downtown — or take
the heavy iron steam engines
pulling the troop trains
the generation before mine,

24

Take
the slow shifting of sameness,
the drift of Andromeda in the high dome —
the glittering trash of spent rockets in low orbit
thousands of feet above me, take it all
and tell it to my children
who tonight sleep in their beds at peace
while I in middle age stare at the ceiling,
frozen against an empty prayer,
4 a.m., 1988, the switch engines running,
the engineer tapping the whistle
the signal for the switchman to throw the lever;
then as the train rumbles by,
making its switching run, the switchman
steps onto the ladder and comes aboard — somewhere
down the track the powerful headlight beam
finds a bend in the dark — the track swings
west and lifts its long narrow burden
onto the high plains, and a hundred villages later
the stock market will crash
and the railroad will have a layoff —
3 a.m., you can find the old engineers and switchmen,
overalls and big heavy hands,
at Dunkin' Donuts along a strip of franchises
built on the land where federal soldiers
fresh off the farm and doomed to Shiloh
camped 120 years ago under Orion more erect — take

The Good News (if you can find some)
and tell it to my children; tell them
what you always do, that it's shelter
from the ravages of evil, and reversals of time —
tell them early and often, so they don't forget
in some lonely night

when the hard steel sound of switch engines
invades their prayer
and they find themselves limited to listening
to the lives that don't sleep,
to trains, and to traffic
out on the night streets — the wide rough world
spilling toward them in their beds
in their little towns.

OLD PICTURES OF ME

I've outlived three generations
of concrete on I-57
and the old pictures of me
are fading.

Is it a given that we outlive trees?
There are the sycamores my father set out,
the fresh mounds of dirt at their base.
And in the little shadow of one,
there I am in my baseball cap,
age nine, a big future in management.
In this one, if the shirt was red before,
it's green now, and if there was
ever a soul behind the eyes
it's fled. Perhaps it's in the drawer.
Here's one where I don't know who I am.
Here's one with a crucifix.
Here's one expressly for posterity,
even a notation on the back,
a signal forward to some future me,
if and wherever I might be.
During the time of this one,
I was telling all lies,
and I look slighter than I recall.
Here's my preoccupied and worried slump,
arm slack on a woman's shoulder —
and look at her,
lumpy, blue, ready for anything.
What image was I pursuing here?
What deception was running underneath?
Here, behind the smile,
I wish I'd have known more
yet I don't know how I could have.
My boys sit next to me in this one.

Mike's first-born worried squint
foretold a lot. Dan waves hello
and look at that, just like my father —
in the eyes, bend of the back,
curve of the hand.

Was I evil all those years, or
was I just slow to understand?

TWO

SHONEY'S

To my mother
places like this were great progress
     Carly Simon in an endless rendition
     on the muzak
     a subliminal message piped in on the lower registers:
     Eat fries, eat fries.
The apples are shiny but soft
and the yellow tile floor is slick from the noon mop.
A waitress smiling
     seems to say
     in her sad subtext
     don't worry; I'm worth nothing.

It's midafternoon and the bleu cheese
and the ranch at the salad bar
taste a lot alike
     and Mom, with four weeks to live,
     once she catches her breath,
     is happy as a clam.

Her generation is here.
WWII vets and their wives
trekking in from the interstate —
we're near the outlet mall.
Their rich rural past was bled out of them
as they ardently clawed for the middle.
They gave it up, they would say to us,
for each other and the Buick in the parking lot
and the boom-tide of lemmings they begot.

In the next booth a foursome sits eating club sandwiches
     and one of the women says,
     looking toward the window,

how the sky here is not as good as
somewhere else she's remembering,

that was a special sky,
and the old man next to her
pushes up his glasses
and, elbows in the water rings,
rubs his eyes to hide tears.

"So," my mother smiles, opening her menu,
"isn't this fun?"

THE HAWK

for Russ Kesler

From this angle,
a window in a glass office building's fourth floor,
nightfall comes early in the trees to the east.
Evening brings a stillness,
like how the moment hangs in the air
just before the school bell,
and there's this hawk that visits —
across the windows a shadow flits,
and then I see the animal himself,
going away,
tail fanned and wings wide,
maneuvering slow and careful
toward the dark woods
and his favorite perch.

This is an island of forest in the city,
the city's blowing papers caught at its edge —
junked-up life for which
this hawk was not evolved.
From his perch: the Burger King
and Lutheran Church,
the parking lot, the landfill.
At the exact moment of sundown,
he rises big off the high limb
and with a regal pull of his wings,
heads north toward the Wekiva
and something he remembers.

STREAKS

Then
we looked at pictures;
later
animations;
and now it's come to
long celluloid streaks of
trashy action, pictures a dime a dozen,
the focus on the Far Beyond,
where we're supposedly going.

Or maybe there's no focus or moment —
it's all frantic, relative and inflated,
time speeding up,
death of the particular.

Of course
there's terror and frustration to deal with,
the rush overwhelming;
and we're not all astronauts.
The brain, ever elastic,
accommodates
the surreal streak
and adjusts to the whine of acceleration,
but the heart, quiet and blind
except to rhythm and the real
— thump — thump — thump —
the heart, bless it,
still tries to absorb the moment it needs,
to stop time,
still searches in the long streak of chaos
for the picture.

BASEBALL

I love how close the camera can get.
Do me a favor. Only focus on one thing,
for now — the moment of the switching,
glove to hand.
The ball sails in from somewhere
and it is in the glove. Watch close.
Zip, bare hand disappears, then quick
the ball is on its way again.
Watch, over and over, the lightning
switch. It is never thought about. Catching
is thought about. Throwing is thought about.
Hitting is thought much about.
Watch the ball shift from glove to hand,
a micromoment, conjunction
between catch and throw,
bridge between receiving and giving,
hands and game,
self and other.

WORKING LATE

Midnight, out the front doors, at last.
In the day, there was sun and later
an astonishing storm with two hours of rain.
Still, tonight, stars and sprinklers.
One sprinkler head, by a far light pole,
drives a column of water straight up;
another blindly waters the street.
Puddles sparkle, amble
toward the storm drains. Beyond my car
now alone in the big lot, darkest shadows.
During the day, with its opposite weathers,
most of us came and went. I worked late
and now my light and rain
come manmade.

DIARY OF A DEAD PEOPLE PLEASER

for Daniel

Here's the cow you ate
and the horse you rode out on,
and here's the money you made
and the girls.
Here are the dogs that loved you.
And here's the weather, and the family,
and the work you endured
and the secrets you had in your heart.
Here are quiet complaints
and things you should have said but didn't.
And finally here are notes obscure of origin
and reference
like you knew I'd be here doing this some day.

How you lived your life
they'll tell you,
was your choice;
Death, that big worst-case version of losing your job,
was not.

Here are the lessons:
The undertaker never laughs
at our witty epitaphs and
there is way less love in this life than they're saying,
way more habit.
In your most dreaded dreams
you could not have lived more perfectly
the way you were destined.
Never once did you raise your voice
and there's not a page here where you made a choice.

Sweet dreams, goodbye, I'm tired of worrying about it.

Two dogs under a yellow moon
trot past your flat headstone,
one to howl and one to bark.

Beyond gone,
you're older now dead than you were alive.
But your son's still up here in the dark.

THE END OF THE FATHER

There's ice again on the winter-gray grass,
and the trees are stone cold
and the high red light from the Dixie Truck Stop
is all the light I've got.
There's a rabbit among the headstones,
silent and still, and back against the old road
there's a shadow I can't identify.
There's another road under this snow somewhere,
how the hearse gets from here to there.
There's an owl, or something, in the shadows overhead
washed in the black of winter and the red.
What am I doing here anyway, in Illinois
in the winter in the middle of the night?
My father's headstone is here somewhere.
I should know —
but I can't find it in the snow.

After the wreck
Tack Green, the undertaker, sold us a plot
and a headstone which would lie flat
so it was easy to mow.
It was summertime, thirty years ago.
That day in the sales room of the morgue,
I really did wonder, trying to think of something else,
how long it would be
before Tack Green himself, hefty and red-faced,
would be lugged out here in his own ambulance
black as coal
and dropped waxy and stonefaced like the rest of us
into a hole.
There's a dream I have that comes day or night;
it's a sound dream, the sound of my father's wreck,
a wild skid, the metallic smash and spray of glass.
So fast and then silence, like the silence out here.

I try to listen deep into that dream, peer into it
like I peer into that shadow along the road,
listening terrified for what I've never heard —
the ghost whisper of my father's last word.

Tonight I can't find his headstone;
it's under ice among other stones
in the area of the era of headstones lying flat.
How long did that last? Well,
I do see Tack Green's stone jutting up
a few rows over which, row by row,
in the cadence of how graves in our town go
would mean eight years or so.

FOSSILS

Down in the glen
where Bill Adkisson
found the trilobite in 1958,
at the source of a primal river
within a mile of his house,
you could hear U.S. 45 — Illinois.
Even above the hush of waving corn,
the tassels flirting with the bees,
you could hear the tires on concrete,
farmers winding out their Farmalls
as they crossed the road,
the travelers passing through
in heavily chromed Fairlanes and Electras.
Bill's dad ran the local airstrip,
and you could hear spray planes
banking out over the fields
and swinging in to land —
you could hear it all
from that quiet glen, curled
at the whim of the river into the quiet middle
of a half-mile section
of steaming half-grown corn we called "The End" —
we'd spend the afternoon there,
making plans.

He found it
among the rocks
that collected on the bank
when the water was higher —
it was encased in stone,
a perfect specimen.
You have to wonder how that place sounded
the day the trilobite died —
since then we've had

a glacier and a hell of an earthquake.
Maybe even the whisper of that old river
came later.

Now I'm in a cemetery, some noon, 1986,
age 40 and looking for quiet,
and across the street north
is a clinic where shrinks work,
serviced by a busy three-lane street;
and to the east beyond palms and cypress
drones Interstate 4, backbone of Florida.
The sound from that crazy road
is amplified crossing the manmade lake.

These sounds aren't like the lazy hack-hacking
of distant tractors borrowing the highway
to scramble from field to field —
they're the sounds of men and women who live alone
murmuring to themselves in traffic,
rushing in small cars between day-care
and their jobs.

And above I don't hear the drone of
the ghost of
John Stoop's Waco
lazily setting in just above the wires
and dropping onto the grass strip
so he can catch lunch with Skeeziks at the hangar
but instead 737's high, aligned
on Runway Outer Four, International Airport —
sounds of steady commerce,
the management class, pure paper,

like a storm,
building,
building, and

Bill
didn't plan
to get half killed in Thailand
and again later to nearly lose a leg
in a motorcycle wreck in Texas,
and I didn't plan to work in that glass building
I seek shelter from in this sad place.

The woman buried here last week
had many friends
whose flowers wilt on her grave today.
The man next to her
doesn't share her name —
she's buried
forever in the ground, closer to him
than she might have been willing to stand
while waiting for stamps at the post office —
who knows,
in the clatter and crunch of things now,
whose dead profile staring up we'll rot beside,
whose blood will mix with ours
when the tap root of the post oak
pries open our shells
and a chance tilt of the land
allows the water through?

MICHAEL AT 12

A child is all the tools a child has,
growing up, who makes what he can.
— William Matthews, *A Happy Childhood*

I know where this is going.
Summer, up at seven, you're in the back yard
with all the tools you can find, and nails
borrowed from neighbors who love you
and wood that was left over
from an old attempt to build a soccer goal —
you're building a club house out of plywood.
You remember the one
at the other house, back when you were eight.
By God, this one will have shingles and a floor.
You can imagine, imagine the wonder
that will come from your work —
a chimney maybe, a door on hinges —
you can do it if you try.
You're twelve, after all.

Your hat's a little sideways
when you come in for Gatorade around ten,
and between eleven and noon
you're handsawing like a madman
half a mile of split pine you rescued
from a scrap heap
where they're throwing up a tracthouse in The Cove.

In the afternoon, friends have joined you —
tasks are divided and the project's gone crooked
— maybe a boat and not a club house.
Okay call it a shelter,
and forget the floor —
we should have done that first.

But it's got a window,
and Ryan brought small chairs,
and for a few hours as the sun's going down
you've got something *like* a club house
though by then you know
it isn't perfect and it won't last long
and there's a disappointment in your eyes.
The joints don't fit right,
the tools aren't perfect,
your friends don't want it like you do.

I watch your eyes.
My boy, I love your optimism
more than my own life, by far.
How can I build for you a shelter
that will hide from you the sad adult secret
that nothing you want is very easy
and nothing you can imagine even
in the orange light of this recent disappointment
can show you the depths of hard.

NORTH SHORE REFLECTIONS
(THE ASTRONOMERS)

Your bafflement was never what I wanted;
in those days, I wanted more than that,
when we were strolling along the North Shore
but were basically uninvolved with it,
and I would stop to look
through one of the telescopes the lakefront people
would bring to the Oak Street beach,
and I would peer far, far, far down the great shore
at some girl in the crowd I couldn't even see with
      the naked eye.
Privately I'd fall in love with her
      in the telescope;
I was afraid I'd lose her if I moved.

And maybe I lied to you, by never saying
how much detachment was a part of me;
you would stand next to me and wait, near the men
who were playing chess in the shade
who were watching you when you weren't looking.

The girl in the telescope made small movements,
adjusted her sunglasses on her water-slick face,
lifted one knee, checked the bra of her two-piece
      to be sure, tuned her radio.
From a mile or more away I watched
through some old guy's terribly powerful telescope
while over my shoulder he talked
      about the fish floating ashore,
      THAT was the summer, the dead fish

who'd found their way
down the St. Lawrence and into the Lakes,
choked on the fresh water and washed ashore in the millions —
a natural disaster the old man said.

After a while I let her go,
and I panned the bank of steel lake-front apartment towers,
the curtained, blank, sliding glass windows,
the balconies with 10-speeds and grills and white chairs,
and up in those buildings also were a hundred more telescopes,
as powerful or more than the one I was borrowing —
what terrible, baffling grief preoccupied the astronomers
        of the Great North Shore,
whose longing eye was never ever on the sky,
who panned the beach from dim isolation,
self-whispering.

PINK

From a DC-3 in 1965
at the airport in Champaign
(I walk uphill to find my seat,
the stewardess distributes gum),
I watched my sister, standing at the gate
dressed in pink, I don't know why —
pink,
the only color in a bleached out memory
of damp summer sun and gleaming white concrete.
The weeds incubating along the retaining fence
were breathing all the air there was to breathe,
haze of heat,
haze —
she was trying to find me in the row of windows
to wave goodbye once more —
she couldn't.
I waved and she kept scanning, age seventeen,
too much eye-makeup,
long hair after the style of the time —
I waved and waved but she couldn't see me,
the pilot fired the port engine
and we taxied away.

It was the right kind of goodbye to childhood,
but the pain was in knowing it right then;
goodbye to Illinois, middle of the middle —
goodbye to anything I could ever again call home,
I mean really home — home the place — home the mother —
home the middle of the middle.
We screamed down the long slab
hellbent toward flying
until finally the ground tilted away
like life in a dream about dying, and

we banked into a turn;
we were fairly high by then,
and vibrating to the tune of the engines,
but looking down through haze
I suddenly saw her,
I could see her there,
see her, there,
pink dress, very small,
hurrying across the parking lot to the car.
Mother of Mercy. I was gone.

ADULTHOOD

My son quit his job today,
dead set on his own beat and drummer,
the far end of nothing not in sight
and only himself to blame.

We celebrate year after year
how the grand scheme favors us
without a thought as to how
it might favor us more

if we could frame our youthful dreams
in some reality other than the one
we were given by our deceased fathers
who, looking down, think they know better,

and, in a way, they do
but, in another way,
like our complacent guardian angels,
only hold us back.

BODY FOUND BEHIND THE 7-11

This is not the kidnapped 7-11 clerk,
from the store one hundred yards away, no —
this is *yet another* victim,
no record of her being OR her being gone.

We know it isn't the 7-11 clerk
because this skeleton has rings
and breast implants. Comedy.
Among the bones of a dead woman,

weathered silicone bags
unbiodegradably lay helter skelter
along her backbone where they landed
when they fell through. Yup,

here's the latest proof
that you can't take it with you —
we biodegrade at multiple rates,
a woman's breasts in a matter of moments

after the warmth leaves, bones four years later
if you have good winters, teeth a century after that;
processed silicone — well —
in plastic it grows cloudy when refrigerated

but constitutionally it has a half-life of
six hundred times the length of the Vietnam war.
Do we ever think when we're adding on
how these silly additions will outlive us?

Happiness upon happiness. Shadow upon shadow.
Running scared, with a half life of twice
life's tears and quadruple its deteriorations —
it's no wonder the shadow who killed her was confused.

VALUJET

I'm glad that plane completely disappeared
with a big brown splash
straight into a mud bog, goodbye.
And I'm glad they all went together.
I'm glad it didn't level off, skip once
and at 350 miles an hour
disintegrate in a fiery ass over appetite.
I'm glad the press
couldn't get there from here
and were left to hover over the marsh
in choppers, radioing down
"Did you find any body parts yet?"

And I know 110 people
who are bone tired of hearing
how safe air travel is compared
to the subway and I-95.
I prefer to think they're intact for the most part,
still in their chairs, in deep deep mud
where something shaped like that might
slide quite nicely, in.
A moment before the Nantucket sleighride
they were fine. If there was a bump or lurch,
they thought little of it. Later they were thinking,
looking down on the skim of clouds,
"Surely not today, surely not."
Intact, yes, I choose to think that,
but make no mistake, they died —
the stop was fast —
the Everglades have a lot of mud,
but between the mud and hell there's
limestone, Valujet's one rightful piece of the planet.

PARIS, TN, AUGUST 14

Here, this morning,
I unload an hour of sadness
standing at the curb in a southern neighborhood
watching a giddy watchdog
watch me.
The house he guards
has a Nerf football,
aged and returning to sponge,
trapped under the eave
of the tin roofed porch
and a rusting bike in the side yard
like a piece of the past
you can't bring in.

My sons are sleeping,
guests in the home of my friends,
in this other house over here.
I've gotten them far from home again — in fact,
with me they've moved on many times,
and now they feel the first knife edge
of the habit of my regret.
It works on them like a ghost.

Along this concrete street
in shadows sharp with the promise of the day
are the South's full range of wood houses,
sheds, and fences, dank and mossy,
flowers as borders leading you back to gardens,
the whole thing always foreign to me and me to it.
In the rising heat the vegetables buzz,
and far off I hear the first car puzzling
through an intersection.

The boys sleep,
and I wait, motionless in this first light,
hoping time won't notice me,
breathing in deeply
the last of my summer.

SEASONAL BLUES

I have one
and I know how to use it
and I can tell you that it does me good
to contemplate it sometimes —
silent in its secret drawer
under double lock
yes separated from its rounds
but poised.

It does me good
to know I have an option
even when it might appear I don't.
Here is your change of game,
your aspirin and your good night's sleep,
for when the blue drizzle
finally turns to rain.

THE LIGHTNING

How these nights it
      tears a crack across the sky
and the birds lay low —
how these nights, in parks and parking lots,
      it occupies the upper half of the dark vision,
      hot and electric
      like these chances we take.

The bushes move. The streets shine.
The rain taps on the car roof.
Lights of a passing car
      spook a shadow into running.

And you — not long after the appointed moment —
      pull up and come to me.
Brightest eyes, a smile.
You take off talking like we'd been together
these last many hours.
You, your light and your light touch
      tear a crack across my heart,
      hot and electric.

WITH YOU

I'm with you always
        is why after 20 years
        I don't sound surprised
        to hear your voice —
I'm with you, hard to explain,
        in some kind of spirit way,
        the memories stretched
        along a ridge of time
As brightly as
        light on a mountainside, no burden,
        and what is time anyway
        but a fine conductor of memory
Like this 3,000 miles
        of glass fiber and spun copper
        conducts your voice in all its softness
        and frightening funny edge —
Time means nothing
        looking back,
        like, though a flower arrests your heart
        in its springtime eruption and blaze,
Really, its fading
        means nothing —
        I'm always with you
        I think because
Once, for just a moment,
        we died into one another
        like a flower dies into the ground,
        at once a small death and,
By an accident grander
        than the sum
        of its lost or fading parts,
        a resounding primal promise.

WOMAN OF DOORS

The woman of the door that's white
is sleeping in a square of light
waiting for the woman of the door

that's blue — she comes when the sun goes.
She uses windows as I use you,
for shelter and to get light through; and

because the woman of the door that's white
is sleeping, because she sleeps alone,
because she is not yet old

but the children are gone, her door is closed;
her hands, beneath the window, cupped,
half-holding the warm sun, are my mother's hands.

And I, her son, am waiting with her in a different place
for the time to pass; her house and mine have
different sounds, doors open, pipes are bumped.

Far apart we listen together for an arrival, someone
from our common past. Who? Night has a shelf
of dark like shoulders of a stranger, moving,

lingering in the yard, wanting in.

THREE

COVENTRY COURT

Is this where I lived back then?
And drove home along this street
    in a near blind routine
    past these trees and graying fences
And daily waved at the jogging
    and walking neighbors
    their familiar faces hell bent?

Back then — way back then — this dust
    of change was only gradually settling,
And time flowed through me
    like alternating current
    and "now" blurred and became
    some former year

And I, preoccupied, floated here
    among these earnest families
    barely attaching myself,
    a ghost already.

STORM

In this town,
the storm's in a different stage.
I've driven back under it, coming from your house in the night.

The drive is
eight minutes linear,
but there's a veil I pass through.

In your town,
it's worth it, doing what I want.
In this town, the rain is relentless.

SABBATICAL

Fall, and the leafy treetops wave.
I have four good watches,
plus my father's, with his blood on it.
That's a lot of time.

THE WORRIERS' GUILD

Today there is a meeting of the
Worrier's Guild,
and I'll be there.
The problems of Earth are
     to be discussed
     at length
     end to end
     for five days
     end to end
     with 1100 countries represented
     all with an equal voice
     some wearing turbans and smocks
     and all the men will speak
     and the women
     with or without notes
     in 38 languages
     and nine different species of logic.
Outside in the autumn
     the squirrels will be
     chattering and scampering
     directionless throughout the town
     because
they aren't organized yet.

THE HOUSE DOWN THE STREET

With dark red brick that went black
at the end of the day, blank windows
that gave you not a thing.
With a broad front porch of chilly stone,

visible through it,
a dank living room, still in the dead light,
edge of a corner staircase that equipped
the dusty parlor for retreat.

In the carport a fading Buick
that never moved. Above the drive,
in a small window good for little else,
the model of a sailing ship,

an old idea perhaps or an old toy.
At sundown sometimes
there'd be the clank of dishes.
And always someone would mow the lawn.

It is fact that one night
there was a prowler;
he accessed the master bedroom
through a window from the roof.

I've had the dream both ways —
seeing the silhouette outside as he sought
his way in; seeing only darkness inside
and wanting to turn back.

Who was this prowler anyway
but the insistent encroachment of the curious?
And who were these people so resolute
to lock us out?

CORONA

This morning I've taken
my grandfather's magnifying glass
and through it eyed in specific
the edges and stared into the metallic black
and closely noticed the archaic curves and
followed the rigid up-down vintage old gold decal
across the face of his typewriter.
Corona.
Everything's big,
and the smell of the oil is still there
and the metal filings from the wear.

Nevermind what I was looking for,
key by key, I looked.
The E and D were worn but
the spacebar had an indention
from a quadrillion light touches of the thumb
as though space was what we needed most.
I climbed higher, found the carriage,
huge, like a train parked on a siding.
Then from there I could see
into the open well,
the dark ribbon and armatures and linkages,
the mysterious action, shift and slide,
gray metal and inner workings,
a perfect extension of my grandfather's
long-deceased desire to express himself,
enormous,
like staring into a cooled-down crater
and seeing far below
a whole factory
occupying
the center of the earth.

SUGAR

There it would be again, in the sugar,
the Sign of the Cross,
one last holy detail from some holy finger
that then receded into the labyrinth of gleaming hallways
and private unseen rooms, folded in upon.
From my chair, I could see down the shadowed halls.
The wood floors shone from the toil of devotions.
In my honor, Sr. Columba convened these dinners.
We ate in a special room —
I, single, 22, current darling of the Dominicans,
the new young teacher in the school across the road;
they, in full black and white habit,
selected from the flurry of two hundred
in residence who were eating elsewhere.
Now I was meeting them one by one,
shaking their hands, looking into their eyes.
Some were as young as me but they'd chosen Christ,
some were seasoned soldiers in the war of faith.
Some were old, bent, closed, and silent.
On dark wood paneling between tall windows
hung a life-size crucifix, guarding their virtue,
intimidating them and watching my every move
(he might as well have stepped down from the wall
for asparagus and potatoes and tea).
There was never a meal prayer like this one,
Columba in her starched habit, that framed
her gorgeous face in white,
taking the hands of her sisters left and right,
and so on down the line, storming her invocation
on an errand of thanks be to God
for this food we eat and these lives we lead together.

Whichever one she was,
I can imagine the force that pushed her,
like being born again,
and I know what she'd call that force
and it wouldn't be pretty.
One day I checked my mailbox between classes.
There was a small card, in an immaculate white envelope.
In delicate handwriting but unsigned it said:
"Tell no one that I've written you. Please come again.
I'm the one who blesses the sugar."

ILLINOIS

I recall a catbird on the wire
between my house and the corner pole
and the dense green maple leaves
and the grass growing fast below
and the peonies, tulips, the sidewalks
stretching down each block to my friends,
and from out of the houses, the voices
of neighbors camped nearby for life,
those close to us in spirit,
those held at arms length, and they us,
and I know when I recall this bird
dancing on our phone line and
singing upwards toward a mate
invisible in the waving treetops,
that it isn't exactly the bird I'm remembering
but the slant of light and the swell
of humid Illinois summer
pressing in around her.

NEW YEARS

In the Florida wind, the new year comes,
not on the same day it came last year —
see how New Years changes
when it's on Friday,
and how that next Sunday changes too?
A rigid grid of days of the week
rides upon the back of the year's calendar,
like a full pack shifting on a wobbly mule.
Our dreams of the new time are prospective
and fresh, and for the moment our old habits
lay low.

TIME

In traffic today, a Buick Wildcat,
white, 1962,
pulled up at the stoplight next to me.
This was a big car.
And oh how I remember ours.
The steel in it was impervious,
it was big and aggressive,
zero to sixty in a neck snap,
and it shined and overwhelmed with its
newness and relative grace.
Surely civilization peaked
in 1962.
So today at the light I looked closely,
to see whether this specimen —
ours being long gone —
was burning oil, and where the rust
in 35 years had finally settled.
I could see it was carefully maintained,
unlike the balding driver, Grecian Formula apparent,
cigarette in his reddish puffy hand,
God you can't stop time.
The metal under the vinyl roof
was soft around the Buick emblem,
and the interior of the front wheel wells
was revealed in fact to be plastic.
The chrome, they used a lot of chrome then,
the chrome in the tail lights had settled
from the metal leaving dark gaps —
maybe rubber had formed that boundary, long gone —
and the big steel back-bumper
was no longer parallel to the road.

Something made me think.
I cranked my rear view mirror
so I could see the man sitting alone in my seat.
What had happened to me in the time it took
to wear out a Wildcat?
The high school sophomore in your face,
I noticed suddenly,
isn't where you think he is
and what's gone when
he's gone
isn't what you expect.

Paul Newman's in a new movie,
playing the 70 year old that he is.
A close look at the promo picture
and I can see even further downstream.
Aging is very subtle. Not that it isn't also
brutal and telling. But the impact is
oddly placed. Resist it here, to no avail.
Bolster here, take care here, no matter.
Time empties us on the myriad of unguarded
fronts, no matter what we do
and, just when we look away,
on the guarded ones too.

WAITING

I know the place in this new yard
where the day lasts longest —
it is up against a fence,
across the dry November lawn from the door,
past the end of the sidewalk,
beyond the garage and the yard light.
I have a fine plastic chair to move there,
and my notebook to bring if I need it.
And the air is good too
and the gray fence is sun warmed.
In the blue drizzle of an impending mood
I can wait and not be seen if I cry.

On this day my daughter's with her boyfriend,
on this one her friends have dragged her to the mall,
this other time she's tooling home alone from practice;
anyway,
most days she's driving, my lovely, open little girl,
nearly grown, out in the Florida swarm and jam,
without me.
Surely she has questions.
The evening will bring her home,
not to my home, for a warm dinner not my dinner,
but maybe later she'll come by,
scoot in the driveway, scatter of headlights,
clatter of barking dog —
maybe she'll know I'm waiting,
maybe in the house in my chair with a book
like I'm reading,
or maybe out here by the yard fence in the last light —
chill of shadows. You stupid shit, yes,
the day lasts longer here, but not *that* much longer, and
have the jays been around all day
and only now their scolding comes to mind?

SOLSTICE

Last night,
the lingering of the solstice
made me notice dusk.
I was brooding in my bed,
the sliding screen open to the yard.
The giant schefflera outside was still
and all things God made paused.
Then,
like a note slipped into an envelope,
the day went into evening.
I could feel it go
in the lifting of the chilly air.
When the sun came back up,
seven this morning, the sky
went from gray to pink to blue
and all I could hear were dogs far off.
I got the strong feeling that
we wanted an eclipse, and now I hear
it will come on Christmas.
The earth is rocking on its mythical axis,
the planets are dancing all around.
Life —
a little blood in much water,
a random breeze in the huge, embracing,
fabulous, ironic, resonating, sweet morning air —
doesn't have to be this hard.

THE BIRD STORY

What I'm going to tell you now happened. None of this is made up to sound good. My sister, who was here five days, helped me settle in and clean the place, then left on Friday. I haven't actually spoken to anyone since she left. This kind of solitude is a great gift, and also an odd thing sometimes. I think there is such a thing as emotional intelligence, something quite different from IQ, and I think a hypersocial life like we lead in our towns and our jobs and even our families neglects the emotional intelligence, or allows us to neglect it, in lieu of the more verbal and socialized regular old intelligence that I'll call IQ here for lack of a better term though it is really unsatisfactory but don't interrupt, so anyway, so I was blue this morning, one never knows why, and I got up and cleaned, obsessively, myself and the house, and it was cold but I got the one room warm using the heater and used that to write in (the room not the heater), and then around 12, still a little blue although the writing went pretty good, I stepped out onto the deck, it was about 70 degrees out with 12-o'clock beaming-down sun and I was wearing all black so it warmed me up fast even though the day was windy, and I was sitting out there and took a few deep breaths and started to listen — and there was a bird somewhere in the stand of pines (west of the house), so I went in and got the binoculars, and I came back out, and I sat back down, and I panned deep into the dark noon shadows of the little pine forest there to the west of the cabin, trying to see if my ears would tell me where to point the binos so I could see this bird with its interesting and persistent song but guess what — the damned bird had gone on the other side of the house, had circled behind me into the poplars on the east side between the house and the road. I could still hear him and that's why I knew where he was, but I was damned if I was going around to that side of the house and chase his little flea-feather butt so I put down the binoculars and I sat there listening, staring west and here's what you see staring west: electrical lines, the stand of pines, a vast open space above the valley of the Toe, and the tree tops of the trees in that valley. I just sat there and stared straight ahead, and listened to this bird, resigning myself that he was there not to be seen but only heard, like a red flower, auditory version. I must have listened for ten minutes, and I could feel my heartbeat going down for the first time since I got here eight days ago, and instead of using tools like binoculars, I just enjoyed resting, staring ahead, and letting the bird's song take me. I could tell that he was moving, first from the stand of pines to the other side of the house before I got a chance to see him, then from tree to tree behind me it seemed. I didn't turn around, I just listened, tracked him by his song and that was enough, and I could tell he was moving but it was of no concern to me because I'd given up all hope of seeing him and was only listening and I'd decided that was fine. Then for a few moments I could hear that he was off to my left, and then more forward so that maybe he was even in the corner of my eye, but I wasn't gonna look. I just stared ahead and listened to his persistent and beautiful sound. Then do you know what happened? He flew to the wire directly in front of me. There wasn't a place he could have landed where he could have seen me better nor I him. I was looking straight ahead of me down a tunnel of vista not more than twenty feet wide, and he landed squarely in the middle of it, and faced me, and kept singing, then turned his back as if to show his markings for my later reference in the Bird Book on the table in the house. Then turned back toward me, and sang and sang. I picked up the binoculars, and he let me have a very close look. A beautiful black/brown bird with white tips to the edge of the tip of the tail and a rich brown throat and a song I memorized. Finally he turned and baled off the wire and soared down the sky to the valley, out of sight, out of earshot. I know with my heart he'll be back, know it with my heart and not my brain because intellectually there's no reason why this happened nor why it's so valuable. I felt great all afternoon. I have no idea

whether, where you are, it could mean anything at all to you —
maybe it's just a function of the isolation and forest. I feel like
I've had some sort of visitation. Whatever has happened is
appreciated through feeling, because I feel plenty about it but
have no idea what to think about it.

ALTHEA STREET

Okay, so now the long search for Althea is over.
It was an understated deal in the end,
three blocks long and overly quiet,
a secret kept by a few families.
It was right at the edge of the tide pool,
and seemed not exactly to end
but rather to fade into the black water mud.

You'd been there once.
But you'd talked about it many times,
making the joke about the Navy and the hot time you had in
Jacksonville that last time through,
which you said got a street named after you.

You're not so far gone now that you couldn't still be here.
I've been absent two months before, absorbed by my own stuff.
Always knowing you were up there.
Always knowing I could at least call,
and your voice would be there,
and you'd update me on the old hometown
and sing the praises of the gossips there who kept you well-informed.

Last time we were together for a weekend,
I was staring at you as you talked, and I made jokes and so did you,
but death was with us in the room and maybe we knew it.
The neighbor was over for pictures and asked how you were,
and you said not so good. You were scared, to be saying that,
a private woman folded in on yourself like you were.

You said you were embarrassed, to have it be like this.
That you had been so stupid all those years.
Well. How did we know we'd be treated like everybody else.
Maybe we thought it was worth it, doing what we wanted.

HERE SHE COMES

For Laura

Here she comes,
heart as big as an apple,
the look in the eye from her brothers,
desire to win from Mom.
But my genes, too. She's
becoming herself out there, feeling
out to the finest capillaries
in the sweetest skin
what it's like to be completely her.

I watch. And it's as though
an electric charge passes between us.
She'll lift whole worlds upward
with a spirit like this, and pass
the grand elliptical dream of childhood
to her own hopeful children. I live
in these eyes of hers, in this picture of her
focused heatedly on the finish line.
She'll be whole and good enough to bloom
in this grind of adulthood
and I will crave —
wait in my quiet corner,
watch and wait, expectant,
for one true, full, and understanding
glance my way.

TRAVELER: CLASSIC PROJECTION I

I see you, Traveler. Do you see me?
I'm down here, across whatever lake,
my binoculars steadied on the bridge rail.
I see you — at the dresser. I see you at the mirror.
I was where you are not long ago,
and, once settled and virtually unpacked,
just as silent in my movements,
placing my things where I could see them,
gathering my traveling self into a series
of careful piles on table, dresser, bed.
Other travelers were through the next wall,
at the next window. I was not alone
but I was happy to seem alone. I was glad
to stand at the window and seem to watch
below some different city than before.
I would turn away from me the clock radio
with red digits speaking a different time zone,
and thus, much too late by accident, I might
call someone I knew who lived there
just for company. "Surprise. It's me. I'm here.
Were you asleep?"

I do know your loneliness that you feel you must ignore.
I do know your worry that you would deny.
I think I know what pictures you carry with you
and lay out on the table to think about,
with pen, paper for notes, a small silver flask to help
you handle it. As you know, you aren't in this town
actually but only seem to be. Your suite is nowhere,
neutral and the same. You are becoming that way too —
I know *that* worry comes to mind, quick glance in the mirror,
yikes, quick trip to the potty, wonder what's on the news.

I feel like you imagine me out here watching you,
or someone watching; you are not free in this quiet room
like you need to seem to be. At the window you are still
and seem to see me. Likely, it's your reflection you're looking at,
better than the mirror — it's you in somewhere context,
nowhere's skyline beaming in blue and red the names of banks.
You will pull the curtain soon, and I'll be down here alone.
But even without seeing I'll know your movements.
You'll refuse to pay for a glimpse of two people doing it
on adult TV because of the telling record it will make on the bill;
your loneliness must remain a secret. You'll take no chances,
double lock the door, set your own travel alarm.
You will shower yourself hot and red; you'll expunge
all the lights in somewhere, say goodnight to yourself
and one more shred of your youth and the hope that came with it
there for a while; in the dark your suite will be nowhere;
for hours you'll sleep yourself through some unknown proportion
of your life, the business traveler's sleep of the dead,
your shaving kit nearby, dangling from a nowhere hook
your hangbag with two good shirts; your wallet and watch
on the dresser, your traveler's eyes dotted,
your nowhere t's star-crossed.
In the vast expanse of the Radisson king-size
you'll feel small on your usual side, pillows crimped
in the usual way; you'll hear yourself breathe
your nowhere traveler's breathing sound.

From down here, though I'm all closed out,
I do know your loneliness that you feel you must ignore.
I do know your worry that you would deny.
I know your vortex nowhere future, your seeming
whirlwind loss and past; I think I know
what pictures you lay out on the table.
Whatever is up for tomorrow,

you will seem to do your earnest nowhere best,
why? — because you've been unemployed before.
If only you could see real well half a mile into the dark
the crouched figure in the shadows on the bridge.
Oh Traveler in this nowhere of your journey,
signal me that I'm here and you seem to know it.
I'm not a peeping tom, I'm us, you and me,
a sympathetic audience in your nowhere dream.

FLYING

I have a flying dream,
have since I was a kid.
In it, I remember suddenly
how to fly, something
for some reason I've forgotten;
by getting to a certain place
in my mind, I'm able simply to rise.
I go up only about sixty or seventy feet,
but that's high enough to look down on
my house, the one I grew up in,
in Tuscola, look down on it
and the trees of the neighborhood;
it's high enough to watch my father
from above as he leaves for work,
to see my mother as she gathers grapes
from the backyard arbor,
to see my sister in her pretty dress,
pulling all her friends in our wagon
down the long, new sidewalks,
to see our many dogs over the years —
high enough to see the blur of childhood,
to put my quiet shadow over all of us
early on. In the dream it's a summer's day
and I might sometimes also
be the one looking up, squinting hard
and seeing way high above
birds moving, black spots against the blue.

DIMINUENDO

in memory of William Matthews

November, your month to live and die,
has come on us gray again,
making the wind and ground and sidewalks
harder and meaner than they were,
and Fallujah, we're told, is liberated,
settling into its new destiny as a fine set
for a war movie — guess who wins.
But hold it. Not so fast. Let's see
the view from the satellite.
Sure enough, the collective horde
is eating its way out of the cheap seats
into the polar icecap,
and Earth's spinning faster by a click.
Time and money, that's a laugh.
With the cooling of the Gulf Stream,
how long until the dough won't rise?
This *New York Times* obituary
is only seven years yellowed
but we can see something now
that we couldn't back then.
Gimping for blackberries is over.
The world's better for each of us gone,
even if flurried from the stage too early,
even our best fucking bad-boy poet
with his rhythm and his blues.

THE NIGHT LIGHT IN THE NEW LIFE

At the far end of the house tonight
the night light idles on a strange table
in its own amber and shadow.
It has no job to do
except to warm a corner and
indicate that we seem to be here.
Asleep at dark's margins
we strangers in the back rooms
cultivate our own illusions.
That we own this place and live full lives here.
That we are doing fine and are sleeping well.
That we could hurt you
if you broke in to find out
how fine and *how* well.
In the new life, God does seem to be
shining down on us in our strange beds
but there's an odd torment
curling around the house
like fog at the rim of a crater or
that doubtful squint at the rim of a lie,
and we lock the doors and one light stays on
so inside we can see
if we want to.

SKYDIVING

Yesterday in the back yard
I noticed the drone of a helicopter
in the southern sky.
I sat in my plastic Adirondak
and had a perfect view
as finally like a mother guppy
the chopper gave birth
to two black dots falling fast.
Gravity works perfectly
pulling us down the sky,
the way destiny pulls us
across the chessboard
or like relativity creates
a dance so perfect to those who are dancing.
One faller videotapes while the other smiles,
then turns one more somersault
before he clutches the ripcord
and opens himself to that pure terrible moment
that he's probably addicted to.

This is a dream we've had —
flying, nevermind what gravity wants;
knowing that
warm mother earth is concrete
when you hit her from this high up;
flying *sort of*, but downward mainly,
your ass in the delicate hands of God,
and Mozart playing.

ABOUT THE AUTHOR

PHILIP F. DEAVER is a winner of the Flannery O'Connor
Award for Short Fiction. His book, *Silent Retreats,* was pub-
lished by University of Georgia Press. He's held fellowships from
the National Endowment for the Arts and Bread Loaf. His work
has appeared in *Prize Stories: The O. Henry Awards* and been
recognized in *Best American Short Stories* and the *Pushcart
Prize.* His poetry has appeared in *The Reaper, Florida Review,*
and *Poetry Miscellany.* He teaches at Rollins College.

THE FLORIDA POETRY SERIES